SO-BZX-043

STATES

ARIZONA

A MyReportLinks.com Book

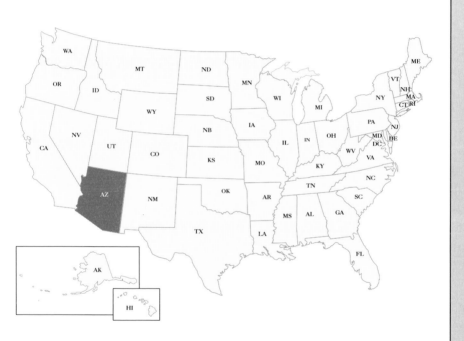

Stephen Feinstein

MyReportLinks.com Books

an imprint of

Enslow Publishers, Inc. E

Box 398, 40 Industrial Road
Berkeley Heights, NJ 07922
USA

MyReportLinks.com Books, an imprint of Enslow Publishers, Inc.

Copyright © 2002 by Enslow Publishers, Inc.

All rights reserved.

No part of this book may be reproduced by any means
without the written permission of the publisher.

Library of Congress Cataloging-in-Publication Data

Feinstein, Stephen.
    Arizona / Stephen Feinstein.
        p. cm. — (States)
    Includes bibliographical references and index.
    Summary: Discusses the land and climate, economy, government, and
history of the state of Arizona. Includes Internet links to Web sites.
    ISBN 0-7660-5023-8
    1. Arizona—Juvenile literature. [1. Arizona.] I. Title. II.
Series: States (Series : Berkeley Heights, N.J.)
F811.3.F45 2002
979.1—dc21
                                    2001006850

Printed in the United States of America

10 9 8 7 6 5 4 3 2 1

To Our Readers:
Through the purchase of this book, you and your library gain access to the Report Links that specifically back up this book.
The Publisher will provide access to the Report Links that back up this book and will keep these Report Links up to date on **www.myreportlinks.com** for three years from the book's first publication date.
We have done our best to make sure all Internet addresses in this book were active and appropriate when we went to press. However, the author and the Publisher have no control over, and assume no liability for, the material available on those Internet sites or on other Web sites they may link to.
The usage of the MyReportLinks.com Books Web site is subject to the terms and conditions stated on the Usage Policy Statement on **www.myreportlinks.com**.
In the future, a password may be required to access the Report Links that back up this book. The password is found on the bottom of page 4 of this book.
Any comments or suggestions can be sent by e-mail to comments@myreportlinks.com or to the address on the back cover.

Photo Credits: © Corel Corporation, pp. 3, 10, 11, 18, 23, 28, 30, 44; Anne Enslow, p. 13; Courtesy of MyReportLinks.com Books, p. 4; Courtesy of ALIS Online, p. 33; Courtesy of Arizona Governor's Office, p. 32; Courtesy of Desert USA, p. 39; Courtesy of Durango Trading Company, p. 29; Courtesy of Gale Group, p. 34; Courtesy of National Geographic Society, p. 20; Courtesy of PBS, Nature, p. 21; Courtesy of PBS, New Perspectives on the West, pp. 41, 42; Courtesy of The American Southwest, p. 26; Enslow Publishers, Inc., pp. 1, 17; Library of Congress, p. 3 (Constitution); Stephen Pecoraro, pp. 14, 37.

Cover Photo: © 1999 Corbis Corporation

Cover Description: The Grand Canyon

Contents

    Report Links. **4**

    Arizona Facts. **10**

1 **The State of Arizona** **11**

2 **Land and Climate** **17**

3 **Economy**. **25**

4 **Government**. **31**

5 **History**. **36**

    Chapter Notes. **46**

    Further Reading **47**

    Index **48**

MyReportLinks.com Books
Great Books, Great Links, Great for Research!

MyReportLinks.com Books present the information you need to learn about your report subject. In addition, they show you where to go on the Internet for more information. The pre-evaluated Report Links that back up this book are kept up to date on **www.myreportlinks.com**. With the purchase of a MyReportLinks.com Books title, you and your library gain access to the Report Links that specifically back up that book. The Report Links save hours of research time and link to dozens—even hundreds—of Web sites, source documents, and photos related to your report topic.

Please see "To Our Readers" on the Copyright page for important information about this book, the MyReportLinks.com Books Web site, and the Report Links that back up this book.

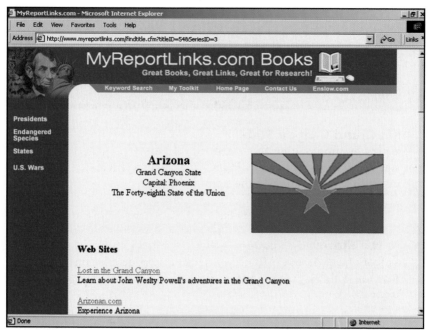

Access:

The Publisher will provide access to the Report Links that back up this book and will try to keep these Report Links up to date on our Web site for three years from the book's first publication date. Please enter **SAZ5186** if asked for a password.

Report Links

> The Internet sites described below can be accessed at
> ## http://www.myreportlinks.com

*EDITOR'S CHOICE

▶ **Lost in the Grand Canyon**

At this PBS Web site you will learn about John Wesley Powell's discoveries during his expedition through the Grand Canyon in 1869.

Link to this Internet site from http://www.myreportlinks.com

*EDITOR'S CHOICE

▶ **Arizona State Parks**

At the Arizona State Parks Web site, you can view maps and descriptions of twenty-eight of Arizona's parks in the northern, southern, and western regions.

Link to this Internet site from http://www.myreportlinks.com

*EDITOR'S CHOICE

▶ **Arizonan.com**

Arizonan.com provides information about Arizona's attractions, towns, history, American Indian reservations and more.

Link to this Internet site from http://www.myreportlinks.com

*EDITOR'S CHOICE

▶ **Arizona: Grand Canyon State**

This site provides information about Arizona's economy, population, sports, state parks, and more. You will also find links to famous Arizonans and information about the state's history.

Link to this Internet site from http://www.myreportlinks.com

*EDITOR'S CHOICE

▶ **Explore the States: Arizona**

America's Story from America's Library provides a brief description of Arizona. You will also find links to stories and information about Arizona.

Link to this Internet site from http://www.myreportlinks.com

*EDITOR'S CHOICE

▶ **The Nature Conservancy of Arizona**

At the Nature Conservancy of Arizona you can explore Arizona's wildlife. Here you will learn about land regions such as the Sonoran Desert, the Apache Highlands, the Colorado Plateau, and the Mojave Desert.

Link to this Internet site from http://www.myreportlinks.com

Report Links

The Internet sites described below can be accessed at
http://www.myreportlinks.com

▶ **Arizona Governor's Office**
At this Web site you will learn about the office of the governor and find the biography of Governor Jane Dee Hull. You will also find a link to "Arizona's Kids" where you will learn about Arizona's history, natural wonders, wildlife, and more.

Link to this Internet site from http://www.myreportlinks.com

▶ **Arizona Guide**
At this Web site you can explore all the regions of Arizona. You will also find an overview of the state of Arizona, a map of the state, and information on all of Arizona's cities.

Link to this Internet site from http://www.myreportlinks.com

▶ **Arizona State History**
At this Web site you can explore Arizona's history, geography, natural world, tourism, and more.

Link to this Internet site from http://www.myreportlinks.com

▶ **Arizona State Legislature**
At this Web site you can take a virtual tour of the Arizona state Capitol building, read the Arizona constitution, and learn about the legislative process.

Link to this Internet site from http://www.myreportlinks.com

▶ **Arizona State Museum**
At the Arizona State Museum Internet site, you can explore their collections and exhibits.

Link to this Internet site from http://www.myreportlinks.com

▶ **Central Arizona Project**
The Central Arizona Project's mission is to allocate water from the Colorado River to central Arizona. Here you will find a link, "Just for Kids," where you will learn about the aqueduct, the aquadrop, facts about water, and more.

Link to this Internet site from http://www.myreportlinks.com

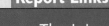
MyReportLinks.com Books

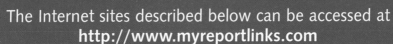

The Internet sites described below can be accessed at
http://www.myreportlinks.com

▶**Discover Southeast Arizona**
This Web site provides an overview of southeast Arizona.
There are links to Arizona's history, outdoor fun, wildlife, and
a photo gallery.

Link to this Internet site from http://www.myreportlinks.com

▶**Discovering London Bridge**
At this Web site you can explore the history of the original London
Bridge, which was was sold to Lake Havasu City, Arizona, in 1970.

Link to this Internet site from http://www.myreportlinks.com

▶**Francisco Vázquez de Coronado**
At this Web site you will learn about Francisco Vázquez de Coronado
and his famous journey in search of the Seven Golden Cities of Cibola.

Link to this Internet site from http://www.myreportlinks.com

▶**Frank Lloyd Wright Foundation**
At this Web site you will learn about Frank Lloyd Wright and his
architectural designs. In particular you will learn about Taliesin West,
Frank Lloyd Wright's home and studio in Arizona.

Link to this Internet site from http://www.myreportlinks.com

▶**Grand Canyon**
At the National Geographic Web site you can take an interactive tour
of the Grand Canyon. Here you will find images, facts, and features
describing the Grand Canyon.

Link to this Internet site from http://www.myreportlinks.com

▶**George Crook**
At this PBS Web site you will learn about George Crook, whom
Ulysses S. Grant placed in charge of the Arizona Territory. In 1871,
Crook waged war against the Apache.

Link to this Internet site from http://www.myreportlinks.com

 The Internet sites described below can be accessed at
http://www.myreportlinks.com

▶**Kit Carson**
In 1863, Kit Carson and the New Mexico volunteer infantry waged war against American Indians living in the Southwest. By 1864, most had surrendered to him.

Link to this Internet site from http://www.myreportlinks.com

▶**The Museum of Northern Arizona**
By navigating through the Museum of Northern Arizona's exhibits, you will find information about Arizona's native cultures, fine arts, diverse climate, and geology.

Link to this Internet site from http://www.myreportlinks.com

▶**Nature: Grand Canyon**
At this PBS Web site you can explore the Grand Canyon, where you will learn about the Canyon's native inhabitants and the Colorado River.

Link to this Internet site from http://www.myreportlinks.com

▶**The Navajo Indians**
At this Web site you will learn about the Navajo Indians who live in the Four Corners region of the Southwest. You will also learn about Navajo life and culture, as well as Navajo artisans.

Link to this Internet site from http://www.myreportlinks.com

▶**Phoenix Zoo**
At the Phoenix Zoo Web site you will be introduced to a variety of plants and animals. You will also learn about conservation, caring for zoo animals, and photographing wildlife.

Link to this Internet site from http://www.myreportlinks.com

▶**Sacred Land Film Project**
The Sacred Land Film Project Web site is a companion to the film *In the Light of Reverence*. This site explores the issues surrounding American Indians and sacred lands.

Link to this Internet site from http://www.myreportlinks.com

Report Links

The Internet sites described below can be accessed at
http://www.myreportlinks.com

▶**Sandra Day O'Connor**
At this Web site you will find the biography of Arizona native
Sandra Day O'Connor, the first woman to be appointed to the
Supreme Court.

Link to this Internet site from http://www.myreportlinks.com

▶**Stately Knowledge: Arizona**
This site provides facts and figures on the state of Arizona. You will
also find links to other resources about Arizona and famous Arizonans.

Link to this Internet site from http://www.myreportlinks.com

▶**Theodore Roosevelt Lake**
Theodore Roosevelt Lake was formed after a dam was built on the
Salt River in 1911. At this Web site you will learn about the history
of the dam, and find a collection of photographs.

Link to this Internet site from http://www.myreportlinks.com

▶**U.S. Census Bureau: Arizona**
At the U.S. Census Bureau Web site you will find statistics Arizona's
people, businesses, and geography.

Link to this Internet site from http://www.myreportlinks.com

▶**U.S.–Mexican War 1846–1848**
The United States went to war with Mexico in 1846. In 1848, Mexico
signed the Treaty of Guadalupe Hidalgo, in which Mexico lost much of
its northern territory, including Arizona. At this Web site you will learn
about the causes and outcome of the Mexican-American War.

Link to this Internet site from http://www.myreportlinks.com

▶**USS *Arizona* Memorial Fund**
At this Web site you can learn about the history of Pearl Harbor and
the USS *Arizona*. You can also take a tour through the USS *Arizona*
Memorial where you will find a collection of images relating to the
USS *Arizona* and the attack on Pearl Harbor.

Link to this Internet site from http://www.myreportlinks.com

Capital
Phoenix

Population
5,130,632*

Bird
Cactus wren

Tree
Paloverde

Flower
Saguaro cactus blossom

Mammal
Ringtail (also called "ring-tailed cat")

Amphibian
Arizona tree frog

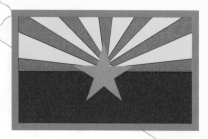

Reptile
Ridge-nosed rattlesnake

Fish
Apache, or Arizona, trout

Population reflects the 2000 census.

Gained Statehood
February 14, 1912

Gemstone
Turquoise

Song
"Arizona" (words by Margaret R. Clifford, music by Maurice Blumenthal);

"I Love You, Arizona" (alternate song, words and music by Rex Allen, Jr.)

Motto
Ditat Deus (Latin for "God enriches")

Nickname
Grand Canyon State

Flag
A five-pointed copper-colored star appears in the center. It represents copper, the state's most valuable mineral. The lower half of the flag is a blue field, the upper half is divided into thirteen equal segments, six light yellow, and seven red. Blue and yellow are the Arizona colors, and red and yellow are the colors of the Spanish, who first came to Arizona in 1540.[1]

The State of Arizona

Arizona, located in the southwestern part of the United States, is a place of surprising variety. When people who live in other places think of Arizona, the first thing that comes to mind is often the Grand Canyon, one of America's most amazing natural wonders. People also think of Arizona's deserts and the retirement communities that attract many senior citizens who wish to escape cold winter weather in other parts of the country. Yet Arizona is much more. At least one-fifth of the state is covered by forests. Snowcapped mountains provide ideal slopes for

▲ A snowcapped mountain in Arizona.

skiing. In addition, Arizona's lakes and rivers offer every type of water sport. Yet the various groups of people who have chosen to live in Arizona throughout its history are perhaps the state's most interesting aspect.

Arizona's Diverse Population

Arizona has nearly five million residents. However, the state is so large that it has one of the lowest population densities in the United States. Most Arizonans live in the cities of Phoenix and Tucson and the surrounding suburban areas.

In the 1800s, prospectors discovered numerous deposits of copper and other minerals in Arizona. Mining towns seemed to spring up overnight. By the early 1900s, many people had come to Arizona to work in the mines or on ranches. Today, Arizona is one of the fastest growing states. Young and old are attracted by the climate, relatively affordable housing, and job opportunities in technology-related companies.

People of practically every race and ethnicity can be found in Arizona, but there are three main groups—Anglos, Hispanic Americans, and American Indians. Anglos are white Americans who are not of Spanish descent. Anglos have been in Arizona since the 1800s. Hispanic Americans in Arizona are mainly Mexican Americans, whose native language is Spanish. About one-sixth of Arizona's population is Spanish-speaking.

Hispanic Americans have been in Arizona for about five hundred years, ever since the first Spanish explorers came in search of gold. Still, American Indians have the longest history of all in the area that is now Arizona.

Various groups of American Indians have inhabited Arizona for thousands of years. Ancient cliff dwellings of

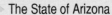

△ *Many people travel to the Canyon de Chelly in Arizona to see American Indian petroglyphs.*

the Anasazi, or the "Old Ones," can be found in Canyon de Chelly, and in many other remote canyons. On the walls of the canyon visitors can see American Indian petroglyphs, or figures cut into stone, and pictographs, or paintings on rock. In the more recent past, Arizona has been home to the Apache, Hopi, Navajo, Pima, and others. Today, the Navajo Indian reservation covers a vast area—more than thirteen million acres—of the northeastern part of the state. The Hopi reservation lies within the borders of the Navajo reservation, and the Hopi and Navajo share some of the land.

▶ **The Grand Canyon State**

People from all over the world travel to Arizona to admire its awesome scenery. The main attraction, of course, is the

Grand Canyon, which gives the state its nickname. Located north of Flagstaff, the Grand Canyon draws millions of visitors a year, mainly during the summer months. The Grand Canyon is truly "grand"—a mind-boggling 277 miles long, 18 miles across at its widest point, and more than a mile deep. Visitors can hike all the way down to the bottom or can take an easier trip on the back of a mule.

Most visitors are at a loss for words when they first see the canyon's vast, silent emptiness and colorful walls of sandstone, limestone, and shale. Many Arizona natives simply refer to the Grand Canyon as "the ditch." The author Frank Waters offered a more eloquent description: ". . . It is at once the smile and frown upon the face of nature. . . . It is Creation."[1]

▲ *Many visitors, like those pictured here, prefer to take a mule ride rather than hike to the bottom of the Grand Canyon.*

There are many other scenic wonders in Arizona. South of Flagstaff, the town of Sedona is famous for its setting in the beautiful red-rock country of Oak Creek Canyon. Also near Flagstaff is Meteor Crater, a gigantic hole in the ground created by a meteorite that fell to earth about fifty thousand years ago. The 570-foot-deep crater is big enough to contain twenty football fields. East of Winslow, the Painted Desert is an area of multicolored windswept hills. In the nearby Petrified Forest, the ground is covered with ancient logs that have been turned to stone by the action of minerals, mainly iron oxide, over millions of years.

On the northern border of Arizona, inside the Navajo reservation, is Monument Valley, a vast expanse of high desert with gigantic sculptured reddish rock formations. Director John Ford chose Monument Valley as the setting for his classic western films *Stagecoach* and *The Searchers*, both of which starred John Wayne.

The Call of the Deserts and Canyons

Over the years, Arizona's beautiful canyons and deserts have inspired artists, writers, musicians, and architects. In 1869, the nineteenth-century American landscape painter Thomas Moran accompanied Major John Wesley Powell on his voyage of exploration down the Colorado River and through the Grand Canyon. In the 1890s, Moran lived and painted on the rim of the Grand Canyon. Frederic Remington, an artist famous for his paintings of cowboys and American Indians, lived and painted in Arizona in the 1880s and 1890s.

One of America's greatest architects, Frank Lloyd Wright (1867–1959), fell under the spell of Arizona's deserts. After several visits, he moved to Arizona in 1937

and built Taliesin West in Paradise Valley near the suburb of Scottsdale. Taliesin West became Wright's western home, studio, and school of architecture. The complex spreads over 600 acres and combines Wright's Prairie Style with elements of the Arizona landscape. Many homes designed by Wright can be found in the deserts of Arizona. Paolo Soleri, an architect who studied with Wright, designed a futuristic, energy-efficient village, a place that would cause as little harm to the environment as possible. Soleri coined the term *arcology* (a combination of *architecture* and *ecology*) and called his dream city Arcosanti. Soleri, with the help of students, began construction in 1970 in Verde Valley, north of Phoenix.

The Arizona landscape has also inspired many writers. In 1908, Zane Grey (1872–1939) built a cabin on the Mogollon Rim, north of Payson. There he wrote western novels that became widely popular. His novels, including *The Call of the Canyon* and *Riders of the Purple Sage*, gave readers a vivid impression of the Arizona landscape. Another writer, Ross Santee (1889–1965), worked as a ranch hand in Arizona before writing realistic stories about cowboy life, such as *Cowboy, Men and Horses,* and *Apache Land*. Santee illustrated his stories with his own drawings of horses and Arizona landscapes. In recent years, Tony Hillerman has written murder mysteries set on the Navajo reservation, such as *Thief of Time* and *The Blessing Way*.

Musicians are also drawn to Arizona. American composer Ferde Grofe's *Grand Canyon Suite* includes a section called *On the Trail*, a musical description of a trip on muleback down the Bright Angel Trail into the canyon.

Land and Climate

With an area of 114,007 square miles, Arizona is the sixth largest state. The northeast corner of the state is known as the Four Corners. Arizona, Utah, New Mexico, and Colorado meet at this point, the only place in the United States where four states meet. Arizona is bordered by New

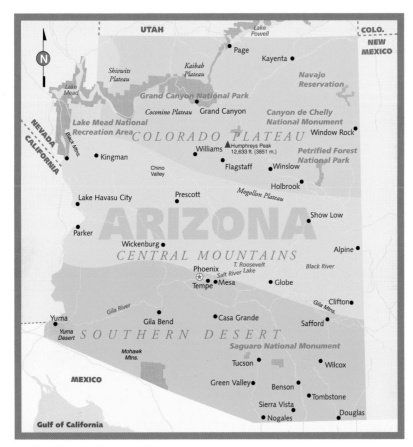

▲ Arizona is one of the states known as the Four Corners. It has three distinct geographical zones.

Mexico on the east, Nevada and Utah on the north, California and Nevada on the west, and the Mexican state of Sonora on the south.

From the Deserts to the High Plateau Country

Arizona consists of three distinct geographical zones— the Southern Desert, the Central Mountains, and the Colorado Plateau. The southern third of the state is mainly desert. The cities of Phoenix and Tucson are located here. This region is also known as basin and range country. Mountain ranges rise from the basins or areas of flat, low desert. These desert basins are a northern extension of Mexico's Sonoran Desert. The basins range in elevation from sea level to about 2,000 feet above sea level. The mountains are thousands of feet higher, such as the

▲ Mexico's Sonoran Desert extends into the southern part of Arizona.

9,250-foot-high Mount Lemmon near Tucson. The desert east of Tucson is a northern extension of Mexico's Chihuahuan Desert. It is a high desert with an altitude of 3,500 to 5,000 feet.

In between the Southern Desert and the Colorado Plateau are the Central Mountains. The highest point in Arizona, 12,633-foot-high Humphrey's Peak, is located in the northern part of this zone. The average altitude of this region is about 7,500 feet. Forests of spruce and ponderosa pine cover the mountain slopes. Those who believe Arizona is nothing more than hot desert would be surprised to learn that the nation's largest patches of ponderosa pine are in Arizona. A two-hundred-mile-long rock cliff known as the Mogollon Rim divides the mountain zone from the deserts to the south.

The vast Colorado Plateau covers the northern third of the state. The average altitude is about 6,000 feet, ranging from 4,500 to 10,000 feet. The Colorado Plateau is actually a series of plateaus, high mesas or flat-topped mountains, separated by canyons. The Colorado River has carved the Grand Canyon through an area of the Colorado Plateau known as the Kaibab Plateau. Much of the Colorado Plateau is high desert, but extensive areas of the mesas are covered by pine forests. Included are the Kaibab National Forest at the Grand Canyon and the Coconino National Forest near Flagstaff.

Water in the Desert

Flowing across northern Arizona is the state's mightiest waterway—the Colorado River. As the river cuts its way across the Colorado Plateau, it continues to deepen the Grand Canyon, a process that began more than five million years ago. The building of Glen Canyon Dam on

Books: Grand Canyon @ nationalgeographic.com - Microsoft Internet Explorer

File　Edit　View　Favorites　Tools　Help

Address http://www.nationalgeographic.com/media/books/grandcanyon/index.html ▾ ⌀Go │ Link

nationalgeographic.com
© 2001 National Geographic Society. All rights reserved.

SITE INDEX ▾

Park of the Month:
Grand Canyon

What and Where
Interactive map, photos, and campsites

Portfolio Grand Canyon
Images of the park

Facts and Features
What makes this park special

In-Depth Insights
Travel into the Canyon

Read More About
NGS Books

Previous Park
Visit Yellowstone

Photograph by Tom Bean

| passport | Books |
© 1996 National Geographic Society. All rights reserved.

Done　　　Internet

▲ *The Grand Canyon, one of North America's natural wonders, is found in Arizona.*

the Colorado River near the Utah border created Lake Powell. The fantastic red cliffs and numerous side canyons bordering the shores of this huge man-made lake suggest scenery on another planet. Thousands of visitors each year rent houseboats and explore Lake Powell and its hundreds of hidden inlets. At the Nevada border, Lake Mead, the largest reservoir in the United States, was formed by the construction of the giant Hoover Dam on the Colorado River. At the Hoover Dam, the river makes a sharp ninety-degree turn and heads directly south, forming the western border of Arizona. The Gila River is Arizona's second major river. It flows westward across the southern part of the state, passing just south of Phoenix before joining the Colorado River.

Throughout Arizona's deserts and canyon country are many seasonal creeks—streams that completely dry up each year due to the lack of rain. When rain finally comes, usually in the summer, it comes all at once. Thunderstorms release enormous amounts of water in just a few minutes. Dry creek beds can become raging torrents, sweeping away anything and anyone unlucky enough to be caught in their paths.

As more and more people settled in Arizona, they started using up the groundwater, the water under the ground. Over the years, an enormous amount of this

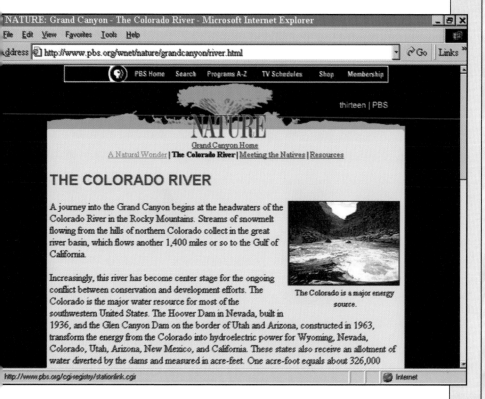

NATURE: Grand Canyon - The Colorado River - Microsoft Internet Explorer

File   Edit   View   Favorites   Tools   Help

Address   http://www.pbs.org/wnet/nature/grandcanyon/river.html

PBS Home   Search   Programs A-Z   TV Schedules   Shop   Membership

thirteen | PBS

NATURE

Grand Canyon Home
A Natural Wonder | **The Colorado River** | Meeting the Natives | Resources

THE COLORADO RIVER

A journey into the Grand Canyon begins at the headwaters of the Colorado River in the Rocky Mountains. Streams of snowmelt flowing from the hills of northern Colorado collect in the great river basin, which flows another 1,400 miles or so to the Gulf of California.

The Colorado is a major energy source.

Increasingly, this river has become center stage for the ongoing conflict between conservation and development efforts. The Colorado is the major water resource for most of the southwestern United States. The Hoover Dam in Nevada, built in 1936, and the Glen Canyon Dam on the border of Utah and Arizona, constructed in 1963, transform the energy from the Colorado into hydroelectric power for Wyoming, Nevada, Colorado, Utah, Arizona, New Mexico, and California. These states also receive an allotment of water diverted by the dams and measured in acre-feet. One acre-foot equals about 326,000

http://www.pbs.org/cgi-registry/stationlink.cgi   Internet

▲ *The Colorado River is a major source of energy to Arizona.*

groundwater was pumped out. People came to realize that at some point, the available groundwater would run out. To make life in the desert possible for Arizona's fast-growing population, it would be necessary to build dams. The Theodore Roosevelt Dam on the Salt River began providing water to the city of Phoenix in 1911. Still, more water was needed. Work on the Central Arizona Project—a system of canals, dams, and pumps, began in the 1970s and was completed in about twenty years. Today, the Central Arizona Project delivers water from the Colorado River to the inhabitants of Phoenix, Tucson, and other smaller towns.

▶ A Dry, Sunny Climate

Many people move to Arizona because of its sunshine and lack of rain. One writer, commenting on Arizona's weather, said, "Umbrellas are considered an oddity in these parts. When it rains, the approved means of keeping water from running down the back of your neck is a cowboy hat."[1]

Most parts of Arizona have close to three hundred sunny days each year. This is about twice as many as in other parts of the country, such as New England, the Pacific Northwest, and the Great Lakes region. In the winter, many residents of cold, snowy parts of the United States flock to Arizona, where much of the state enjoys mild sunny weather. These seasonal visitors to Arizona are often referred to as "snowbirds."

Because Arizona is not close to any large body of water, there is a large variation in temperatures. Winter weather is delightful in the Southern Desert. In Phoenix, for example, the temperature on a typical sunny winter afternoon is between 60° and 70°F. Yet in the mountains and high plateaus in the northern part of the state, winters are often cold and snowy. The North Rim of the Grand Canyon is closed to visitors during the winter. The South Rim, which remains open to visitors, is often covered in snow. Subzero temperatures have been recorded, with a record low of −40°F at Hawley Lake on January 7, 1971.

Summer is an ideal time to visit Arizona's mountains and northern plateaus. High temperatures are usually in the 70s and 80s. Still, summer is not a good time to visit the scorching southern deserts, because some people can be harmed by the intense heat. "People have been known to fry eggs on the sidewalks and let popcorn pop inside closed automobiles."[2] Daytime temperatures are usually well over 100°F. A record 128°F occurred at Lake Havasu City on the Colorado River on June 29, 1994, Arizona's highest temperature ever.

▲ The prickly pear cactus is one plant that thrives in the hot, dry climate of Arizona.

Much of Arizona is desert, which means that there is a scarcity of water. The lowest areas of the southern deserts get hardly any rain at all. Yuma, in the southwest corner of the state, gets about three inches of rain a year. Phoenix gets about seven inches, and Tucson gets eleven. The high mountains get about twenty-five inches of rain a year. Most of the annual rainfall comes during the "monsoon" season—July, August, and early September—in the form of intense thunderstorms.

Unique desert plants that can survive with little water grow in many places in Arizona's southern deserts. The giant saguaro cactus, some of which reach fifty feet in height, can be found at Saguaro National Park in the foothills around Tucson. Organ pipe cactus can be seen at Organ Pipe Cactus National Monument along the Mexican border. The barrel cactus, spiny cholla cactus, prickly pear cactus, and ocotillo are among the other plants that thrive in Arizona's deserts. A variety of desert trees also grow in Arizona, chief among them the paloverde, mesquite, ironwood, and smoke trees.

Economy

Arizona has a rapidly growing economy to match its rapidly growing population. In the past, the state's economic expansion was fueled by the growth of mining—mainly copper and gold—along with the development of agriculture. Mining and agriculture, especially cotton, still contribute to Arizona's economy. In recent years, many ranches have been sold to make way for suburban housing and businesses. Real estate has grown too valuable to be used for grazing livestock. Today, Arizona's biggest industries—tourism and high technology—are thriving. The continued success of Arizona's economy depends on wise use of the state's most valuable resource—water.

▶ Change Comes to the Desert

Without water, people cannot live, work, or grow things. At one time, Phoenix and its desert surroundings, known as the Valley of the Sun, were an agricultural community. The population grew quickly, and a larger supply of water became necessary. This led to the creation of the Central Arizona Project and its system of canals. Agriculture uses a huge amount of water for a relatively small benefit to the economy. Agriculture uses 89 percent of Arizona's water, but produces less than 3 percent of the annual income earned by Arizonans.

As Phoenix and its suburbs spread out over the desert, citrus groves and cotton fields gave way to housing tracts

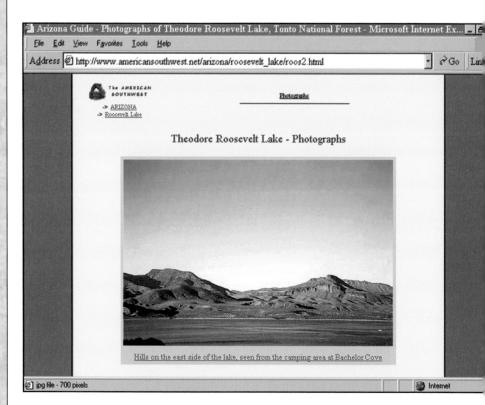

Arizona Guide - Photographs of Theodore Roosevelt Lake, Tonto National Forest - Microsoft Internet Ex...

File　Edit　View　Favorites　Tools　Help

Address　http://www.americansouthwest.net/arizona/roosevelt_lake/roos2.html　Go　Link

The AMERICAN SOUTHWEST

→ ARIZONA
→ Roosevelt Lake

Photographs

Theodore Roosevelt Lake - Photographs

Hills on the east side of the lake, seen from the camping area at Bachelor Cove

jpg file - 700 pixels　Internet

The Theodore Roosevelt Lake was formed by the construction of a masonry dam on the Salt River in 1911.

and manufacturing companies. In recent years, several areas in the Valley of the Sun have decided that future land development will be restricted to housing and industry.

The extent of development has also come into question. Even with the Central Arizona Project, there are limits to how much water can be diverted from the Colorado River. Therefore, there are limits to growth. In May 1998, Arizona Governor Jane Hull, proposed a plan called Growing Smarter. Its purpose was to control growth so that the Valley of the Sun would retain some of its open space. She said, "From day one, I pledged to preserve open space and improve public planning. I want to leave a better place for my grandchildren."[1]

While agriculture was disappearing from the Phoenix area, Yuma, in the southwestern corner of the state, was becoming a more important agricultural center. With a twelve-month growing season, Yuma has become one of the best agricultural areas in the nation. Although special nutrients must be added to the sandy soil, more than 200,000 acres of irrigated land are being cultivated. The main crops are cotton, alfalfa, lettuce, and other vegetables. Cesar Chavez (1927–93), the Hispanic-American leader of the United Farm Workers Union, was born and raised in Yuma. He grew up working in the fields. Later, he fought for better working conditions for migrant farmers.

▶ Silicon Desert

Northern California is famous for its Silicon Valley, the home of thousands of high-tech companies. The high-tech industries have spread to other states, including Arizona. Electronics products such as computers and computer chips, telecommunications equipment, and various kinds of industrial machines are produced in Arizona. South of Phoenix, the town of Chandler has become the center of the new "Silicon Desert." Technology companies such as Intel and Motorola have established manufacturing plants there. Other companies, especially those in the aerospace and defense industries such as Boeing, Honeywell, and Allied Signal, have plants elsewhere in southern Arizona. Companies and their employees benefit from relatively affordable real estate prices. As long as air conditioning is available to assure survival through the broiling desert summer, people continue to enjoy living and working in Arizona.

Fun in the Sun

About 27 million people—more than five times the number of residents of the state—visit Arizona each year. Most visitors are here on pleasure, but many come to do business and to attend conferences. A wide variety of scenic attractions, guest accommodations, and activities are available year round. In the winter, many come to play on spectacular desert golf courses, while others go skiing in such places as Flagstaff's Snowbowl Ski Area or the Mount Lemmon Ski Valley near Tucson. In the springtime, several major league baseball teams hold training sessions in the state. In the summer, millions visit Arizona's scenic treasures such as the Grand Canyon and the other lesser-known canyons, buttes, and mesas. Dude ranches offer a taste of the traditional western lifestyle, featuring trail rides and campfires.

▲ The Organ Pipe National Monument gives visitors a breathtaking look at the Sonoran Desert.

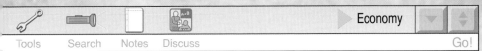

Navajo Life and Culture - Microsoft Internet Explorer

File Edit View Favorites Tools Help

Address http://www.americanarts.com/nlifcult.htm   Go   Links

There is a division among the Navajo of today. Many strive to hold onto tradition while others are swayed to integrate into the white culture. The boarding school experience, the Livestock Reduction Act, the land dispute issues with the Hopi--all splintering the Navajo people making it difficult if not impossible to assimilate traditional ways in today's lifestyle. Some Navajos leave the reservation and in so doing, leave behind their traditional beliefs. For the Navajo, the land is everything--representing the traditions and the culture.

Done   Internet

The Navajo Indian reservation occupies more than 13 million acres of land in the northern part of Arizona.

The city of Phoenix and its surrounding areas host Arizona's professional sports teams. Residents and visitors alike can take in Phoenix Suns basketball games, Arizona Cardinals football games, and Phoenix Coyotes hockey games. Or, baseball fans can watch the Arizona Diamondbacks baseball team, the 2001 World Series champions.

Visitors to the Navajo Indian reservation can learn about traditional Navajo lifestyles. Those interested in history can visit prehistoric cliff dwellings or the Mission San Xavier del Bac, south of Tucson. Built by the Spanish

in the 1690s, the beautiful white adobe mission is known as the "White Dove of the Desert."

Swimming, sailing, and canoeing are favorite activities on Arizona's rivers and lakes. Each year, there is a long waiting list of people hoping to make reservations for river rafting trips on the Colorado River through the Grand Canyon. On Arizona's western border, the building of Parker Dam on the Colorado River created Lake Havasu. A retirement and resort community, Lake Havasu City soon sprang up along the lakeshore. At Lake Havasu City, visitors can see one of Arizona's strangest sights. There in the Arizona desert is London Bridge! Indeed, this is the actual stone bridge that once spanned the Thames River in England. It was taken apart, stone by stone, a total weight of about 10,000 tons, and shipped to Lake Havasu City, where it was rebuilt. Visitors say it must be seen to be believed.

▲ *Many visitors enjoy canoeing on Arizona's rivers and lakes.*

Government

On February 14, 1912, the United States Congress signed papers admitting Arizona to the Union as the forty-eighth state. Arizona had already planned for this day by creating a state constitution two years earlier in 1910.

▶ Arizona's Constitution

The Arizona Constitution outlines the structure of the state government and a bill of rights for Arizona's citizens. It also spells out the various powers of the state dealing with such things as education, public health and welfare, and natural resources. The constitution also describes Arizona's electoral process. The purpose of the constitution was to protect the rights of Arizonans. Unfortunately, at first not every citizen of Arizona had the right to vote. Women gained the right to vote in state elections shortly after statehood was achieved. Arizona's American Indian citizens were not given the right to vote until 1948. That year, the United States Supreme Court ruled that not allowing American Indians to vote was unconstitutional.

▶ The Structure of Arizona's Government

Arizona's government is based on a separation of powers, just like the federal government and the governments of the other states. The Arizona Constitution divides the state government into three branches—executive, legislative, and judicial. The chief executive is the governor, who is elected by the state's voters to a four-year term of

CURRENT EVENTS

ARIZONA

OFFICES OF THE GOVERNOR

COMMUNITY POLICY OFFICE

BOARDS & COMMISSIONS

EQUAL OPPORTUNITY

EXCELLENCE IN GOVERNMENT

STRATEGIC PLANNING & BUDGETING

ARIZONA / MEXICO COMMISSION

K-12 TASK FORCE REPORT

Arizona Homeland Security Information and Resource.

ARIZONA

January 7, 2002

STATE OF THE STATE

CHARACTER COUNTS

STRATEGIC PLAN

INTERN PROGRAM

ARIZONA KIDS

HULL LEADS WGA

"My goals as Governor are to improve education and ensure that Arizona remains one of the most attractive places in the nation to live, work, and raise a family."

▲ In 1997, Jane Dee Hull became Arizona's second woman governor.

office. Arizona's governor has more limited powers than do the governors of many other states. The governor is responsible for seeing that the laws of the state are enforced. Although he or she may recommend new laws and submits an annual budget to the state legislature, final decisions on such matters are made by the lawmakers. Also, the governor has the power to appoint people to state office, but the appointments must be confirmed by the state senate. However, the governor does not have the power to remove such people from office. The other top positions in the executive branch are the secretary of state, the attorney general, the treasurer, and the state superintendent of public instruction.

The legislative branch of Arizona's government consists of the state senate and the state house of representatives. Senators and representatives are elected by the voters to a two-year term of office. Their main job is to propose new laws, mainly laws that protect the safety, health, and welfare of Arizona's citizens. Both houses must then enact an identical proposal before it is sent to the governor for final approval and signing into law.

The judicial branch of Arizona's government consists of the state supreme court; the court of appeals; the superior courts—the basic trial courts of Arizona, organized on a county basis; and the city and other local courts.

▲ Arizona's state capital complex is located in Phoenix.

▶ Direct Democracy in Arizona

In Arizona, the citizens share the lawmaking power with the state legislature in various ways. In the initiative process, citizens use a petition to propose laws that will be voted upon by the people at the next election. If people object to a law passed by the legislature, they can call for a referendum by getting signatures of voters on a petition. Sometimes, the legislature will leave the final decision on a proposed law up to the voters. Arizona's voters have the power to remove any person holding an elected office in the state by petitioning for a recall.

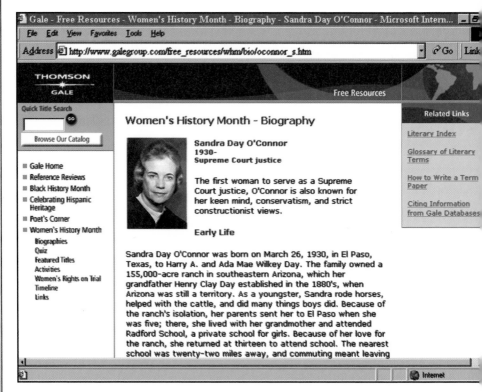

Sandra Day O'Connor was the first woman to serve as a justice of the United States Supreme Court.

Arizona Women in Government

Almost from the moment Arizona became a state, Arizona women played a role in government. Frances Munds and Rachel Berry were elected to the Arizona legislature in 1914. In the 1930s, Isabel Selmes Greenway served in the United States Congress for three and a half years. Polly Rosenbaum was elected to the Arizona legislature in 1949 and held her seat until 1995, a period of forty-five years. In 1965, Lorna Lockwood was appointed head of the Arizona supreme court. Lockwood became the first woman in any state to hold this position. In 1981, Sandra Day O'Connor became the first woman to serve as justice of the United States Supreme Court. In 1988, Arizona Secretary of State Rose Mofford became Arizona's first woman governor. In 1997, Secretary of State Jane Dee Hull became governor of Arizona.

Chapter 5

History

During the last Ice Age, thick glaciers covered much of North America. The sea level was much lower than it is today, and a land bridge extended across the Bering Strait that now separates Alaska from Siberia. Archeologists believe that the first people to migrate from Asia to what is now America crossed the land bridge perhaps as early as forty thousand years ago. About twelve thousand years ago, the first groups of people entered what is now Arizona.

▶ Ancient Arizonans

The first Arizonans, descendants of people from Asia, are referred to by scientists as Paleo-Indians. They lived a nomadic life, following the herds of wild animals. Among the animals they hunted was the mastodon, an early relative of the elephant. The mastodon provided meat, hide, and bones for making food, clothing, shelters, and tools. Over time, many of the large animals became extinct. The hunters then turned to smaller animals, such as rabbits and deer. They settled in caves and gathered fruits, nuts, and berries.

Eventually, people began to experiment with planting and harvesting. About two thousand years ago, a group of American Indians known as the Hohokam were living in villages in the desert south of present-day Phoenix. Today's Central Arizona Project was not Arizona's first extensive system of canals. The Hohokam were successful farmers and eventually built a 600-mile network of irrigation canals to carry water from the Gila River. They planted corn, beans, and squash. Some of their canals are still used by farmers today. The Hohokam disappeared around A.D. 1450, perhaps because of disease or severe drought. In fact, the name "Hohokam" is Pima for "vanished" or "all used up." The Pima may be descendants of the Hohokam.

Other early groups of Arizona Indians, such as the Anasazi, also seem to have mysteriously vanished. A Navajo word meaning "Ancient Ones," the Anasazi settled in the Four Corners area of the Colorado Plateau. By around A.D. 200, they were building cliff dwellings—apartment houses made of stone and mud. The buildings were several stories high, built into the vertical walls of canyons, high above the canyon floor. Magnificent

▲ Montezuma Castle National Monument is located in Camp Verde, Arizona.

Anasazi ruins can be seen today at places such as Canyon de Chelly and Betatakin, on the Navajo reservation. The Anasazi also built communities of stone buildings out in the open, known as "pueblos." The Anasazi were farmers and became skilled at making baskets and beautiful pottery. By around A.D. 1300, the Anasazi had disappeared, possibly because of a devastating drought that lasted for many years. Most likely, after abandoning their communities, they wandered off and joined other peoples.

Around A.D. 1400, two groups of American Indians, warlike nomadic hunters who had wandered south from Canada, began arriving in Arizona. Like the Anasazi before them, the Navajo settled in the Four Corners area. They became farmers and raised sheep, and lived in small houses made out of logs and mud, known as hogans. The other people from the north lived in small groups in the mountains of central Arizona. They did not give up their warlike ways, and lived from hunting and carrying out raids against other native peoples. Indeed, the Zuni referred to them as "Apaches," meaning "enemies." Both the Navajo and the Apache, however, called themselves "Diné," which means "the people—those who are fully human."

Another group of American Indian people, the Hopi, built pueblos atop high mesas on the Colorado Plateau. Believed to be descendants of the Anasazi, the Hopi were peaceful farmers who lived in harmony with nature. To this day, the Hopi still live in their ancestral pueblos atop three mesas and several pueblos on the land below on the Hopi Reservation. The mesa-top pueblo of Oraibi was built by the Hopi around A.D. 1100. It is probably the oldest town in the United States in which people have lived continuously through the centuries.

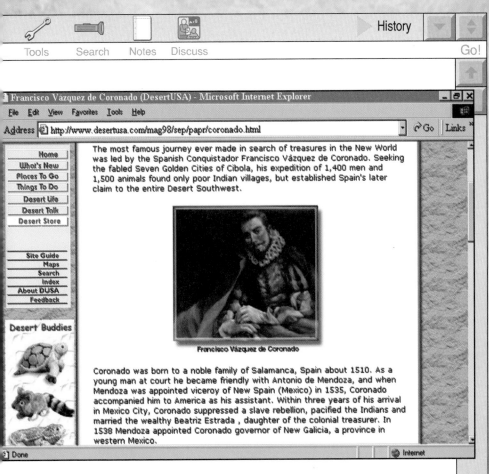

Francisco Vázquez de Coronado (DesertUSA) - Microsoft Internet Explorer

File Edit View Favorites Tools Help

Address http://www.desertusa.com/mag98/sep/papr/coronado.html   Go   Links

Home
What's New
Places To Go
Things To Do
Desert Life
Desert Talk
Desert Store

Site Guide
Maps
Search
Index
About DUSA
Feedback

Desert Buddies

The most famous journey ever made in search of treasures in the New World was led by the Spanish Conquistador Francisco Vázquez de Coronado. Seeking the fabled Seven Golden Cities of Cibola, his expedition of 1,400 men and 1,500 animals found only poor Indian villages, but established Spain's later claim to the entire Desert Southwest.

Francisco Vázquez de Coronado

Coronado was born to a noble family of Salamanca, Spain about 1510. As a young man at court he became friendly with Antonio de Mendoza, and when Mendoza was appointed viceroy of New Spain (Mexico) in 1535, Coronado accompanied him to America as his assistant. Within three years of his arrival in Mexico City, Coronado suppressed a slave rebellion, pacified the Indians and married the wealthy Beatriz Estrada, daughter of the colonial treasurer. In 1538 Mendoza appointed Coronado governor of New Galicia, a province in western Mexico.

Done   Internet

▲ Francisco Vázquez de Coronado led one of the most remarkable European expeditions of the North American interior.

▶ The Spaniards

In the 1500s, the Spaniards arrived in Arizona. They were searching for gold and for souls to convert to Christianity. First to arrive was Marcos de Niza, a Franciscan priest, in 1539. The next year, Francisco Vázquez de Coronado traveled north from Mexico in search of golden cities rumored to be in Arizona. He found Indian pueblos but no golden cities. One of the explorers in Coronado's party, García López de Cardenas, traveled further north and became the first European to see the Grand Canyon. In 1598, Juan de Oñate claimed what is now New Mexico and Arizona as

a colony called New Spain. His attempt to establish the colony, however, was unsuccessful.

In 1692, Eusebio Francisco Kino, a Jesuit priest, began building missions in Arizona, including the Mission San Xavier del Bac south of present-day Tucson. Father Kino and the other missionaries not only taught the Indians about Christianity, but also new methods of farming. However, the Spanish missionaries and soldiers forced American Indians to grow food for them and to build their forts and missions. The Spaniards also introduced European diseases such as smallpox and measles into the region, and many natives died as a result.

Eventually, the natives came to resent the Spanish invasion of their lands and the changes the Spaniards had brought about in their lives. In the mid-1700s, many American Indian tribes, including even the peaceful Pima, attacked the Spaniards, killing many. The Apache, already fierce warriors, stole horses from the Spanish troops and became even more effective at hit-and-run raids. Fighting in Arizona continued through the early 1800s. Then, as Mexico fought for its independence from Spain, Spanish troops in Arizona returned to Mexico to join the fight. Spanish settlers then retreated to the safety of the walled towns of Tucson and Tubac.

In 1821, Mexico won its independence from Spain, and Arizona became a part of Mexico. Mexicans of Spanish descent established huge cattle ranches and became wealthy and powerful. American Indians and mestizos, people who were part Indian and part Spanish, were hired as laborers by the ranch owners. Then, in 1846, Mexico and the United States went to war. In 1848, Mexico, having lost the war, signed the Treaty of Guadalupe Hidalgo, giving away its vast northern territories, including Arizona, to the

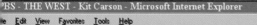

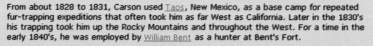

▲ Kit Carson was a famous frontiersman who fought American Indians for their land. His troops defeated the Navajo at Canyon de Chelly in 1864.

United States. In 1853, the United States gained another 30,000 square miles of southern Arizona in the Gadsden Purchase. The signing of these treaties sowed the seeds of new conflict in Arizona for many years to come.

▶ The Wild West

Once Arizona belonged to the United States, Anglos began moving in. The newcomers claimed lands that had belonged to American Indians and Mexicans. The Indian tribes no longer had the right to own or control land. The Mexicans could not prove they held title to their lands. In

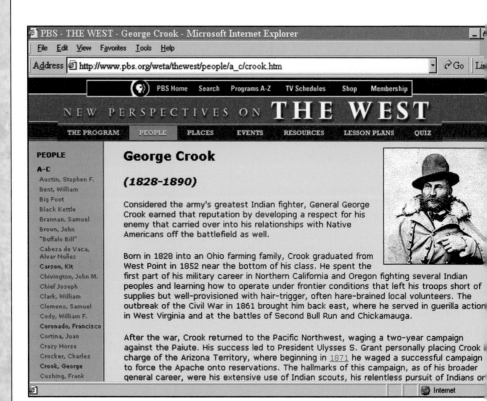

PBS - THE WEST - George Crook - Microsoft Internet Explorer

File   Edit   View   Favorites   Tools   Help

Address http://www.pbs.org/weta/thewest/people/a_c/crook.htm   Go   Li

PBS Home   Search   Programs A-Z   TV Schedules   Shop   Membership

NEW PERSPECTIVES ON **THE WEST**

THE PROGRAM   PEOPLE   PLACES   EVENTS   RESOURCES   LESSON PLANS   QUIZ

PEOPLE

A-C

Austin, Stephen F.
Bent, William
Big Foot
Black Kettle
Brannan, Samuel
Brown, John
"Buffalo Bill"
Cabeza de Vaca, Alvar Nuñez
Carson, Kit
Chivington, John M.
Chief Joseph
Clark, William
Clemens, Samuel
Cody, William F.
Coronado, Francisco
Cortina, Juan
Crazy Horse
Crocker, Charles
Crook, George
Cushing, Frank

George Crook

(1828-1890)

Considered the army's greatest Indian fighter, General George Crook earned that reputation by developing a respect for his enemy that carried over into his relationships with Native Americans off the battlefield as well.

Born in 1828 into an Ohio farming family, Crook graduated from West Point in 1852 near the bottom of his class. He spent the first part of his military career in Northern California and Oregon fighting several Indian peoples and learning how to operate under frontier conditions that left his troops short of supplies but well-provisioned with hair-trigger, often hare-brained local volunteers. The outbreak of the Civil War in 1861 brought him back east, where he served in guerilla action in West Virginia and at the battles of Second Bull Run and Chickamauga.

After the war, Crook returned to the Pacific Northwest, waging a two-year campaign against the Paiute. His success led to President Ulysses S. Grant personally placing Crook charge of the Arizona Territory, where beginning in 1871 he waged a successful campaign to force the Apache onto reservations. The hallmarks of this campaign, as of his broader general career, were his extensive use of Indian scouts, his relentless pursuit of Indians on

Internet

General George Crook is considered the army's greatest Indian fighter. During his last years, he campaigned on behalf of American Indians, speaking out against white intrusion on Indian land.

1863, Arizona Territory was officially established by the United States Congress. Various Indian tribes decided to fight for their lands. In 1864, American troops under the command of Kit Carson defeated the Navajo at Canyon de Chelly.

For the next twenty-three years, the Apache, under the leadership of great warrior chiefs such as Cochise and Geronimo, engaged in a fierce struggle against the United States Army under the command of Major General George Crook. The Indian Wars in Arizona ended when

Geronimo surrendered in 1886. Arizona's American Indians were then forced to live on reservations.

During the years of the Indian Wars, more and more Anglos moved into Arizona. Some came to farm or raise cattle, and some came to mine. A few prospectors found gold and silver. Most miners, though, were drawn by Arizona's huge deposits of copper. Towns were built, and stagecoach routes were established. Arizona lawmen had to deal with cattle rustlers, bank robbers, men who held up stagecoaches, and other types of thieves and scoundrels. Arguments were typically settled with a gun. Gunfights often took place in saloons or on the streets of towns. In the appropriately named town of Tombstone, those who died in gunfights were buried on Boot Hill. In 1881, Marshal Wyatt Earp and his friend Doc Holliday, a gambler, were the victors in the famous gunfight against the Clanton gang at Tombstone's O.K. Corral.

▶ Building a Bright Future

In 1867, a prospector named John W. Swilling was roaming through the deserts of southern Arizona in the area of the Salt River. There he discovered something more valuable than gold or any other metal—the ancient canals of the Hohokam people. "Swilling realized that people could successfully farm the desert. He began dredging the prehistoric ditches, homesteading farmers arrived, and before long what is now the largest city in the state was flourishing."[1] The new town was named Phoenix, suggesting the legendary bird that arose from the ashes to live again after being consumed by fire.

The railroad reached the city of Phoenix in 1887, and the population exploded. Phoenix became the capital of the Arizona Territory two years later. It soon became

clear that the growing city would need more water than the Hohokam canals could provide. The Theodore Roosevelt Dam on the Salt River, a tributary of the Gila River, was completed in 1911. Now the way was clear for Phoenix to grow and prosper. The Central Arizona Project would later bring even more water from the Colorado River.

▶ A Proud State

Arizonans take pride in the accomplishments of the state's outstanding citizens. Ira Hayes, a Pima Indian and World War II hero, helped raise the flag on Iwo Jima after he and his fellow United States Marines captured the island from the Japanese. John McCain, a hero of the Vietnam War who was held prisoner by the North Vietnamese for seven years, became famous as an outstanding United States senator. Equally famous was Senator Barry Goldwater.

▲ Arizona's breathtaking sunsets are a sight not to be missed.

Sandra Day O'Connor became the first woman justice of the United States Supreme Court. In addition, Raul Castro, elected in 1975, became Arizona's first Mexican-American governor.

While Arizonans continue to plan and build a bright future, they also keep old traditions alive. Today Arizonans and visitors to the state celebrate Arizona's rich heritage. The Hispanic culture is evident in much of the state. Mexican restaurants are everywhere, mariachi bands play Mexican music, and there are lively annual celebrations such as Cinco de Mayo (May 5) and Mexican Independence Day (September 16).

The All Indian Pow Wow takes place in Flagstaff. Rodeos take place throughout the state, and remind people of the cowboys who rode the range. Arizona's traditions, cultural and recreational attractions, and scenic wonders continue to provide excitement and enjoyment to all who live in or visit the Grand Canyon State.

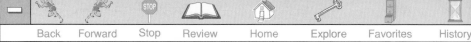

Chapter Notes

Arizona Facts

1. *USA State Symbols, Flags & Facts*, CD-ROM, Canada: Robesus, Inc., 2001.

Chapter 1. The State of Arizona

1. William E. Hafford and Edie Jarolim, "The Grand Canyon and Northwest Arizona," in *Fodor's Arizona 2001* (New York: Fodor's Travel Publications, 2001), p. 34.

Chapter 2. Land and Climate

1. Ray Riegert, ed., *Ultimate Arizona*, Second edition (Berkeley, Calif.: Ulysses Press, 1995), p. 7.

2. Ibid.

Chapter 3. Economy

1. Jane Dee Hull, "Governor Celebrates the Passage of Growing Smarter," *Arizona Governor's Office*, June 1998, <http://www.governor.state.az.us/news/releases/june98/6-12-98nr.html> (March 18, 2002).

Chapter 5. History

1. Ray Riegert, ed., *Ultimate Arizona*, Second edition (Berkeley, Calif.: Ulysses Press, 1995), p. 38.

Further Reading

Cone, Patrick. *Grand Canyon.* Minneapolis, Minn.: The Lerner Publishing Group, 1994.

Filbin, Dan. *Arizona.* Minneapolis, Minn.: The Lerner Publishing Group, 1991.

Fradin, Dennis Brindell. *Arizona.* Danbury, Conn.: Children's Press, 1991.

Gresko, Marcia S., and Lisa Halvorsen. *Letters Home From the Grand Canyon.* Farmington Hills, Mich.: Gale Group, 2000.

Heinrichs, Ann. *America the Beautiful: Arizona.* Danbury, Conn.: Children's Press, 1991.

Joseph, Paul. *Arizona.* Edina, Minn.: ABDO Publishing Company, 1998.

Marsh, Carole. *The Arizona Experience Pocket Guide.* Peachtree City, Ga.: Gallopade International, 2000.

McCormick, Anita. *Native Americans and the Reservation in American History.* Springfield, N.J.: Enslow Publishers, Inc., 1996.

Rawlins, Carol. *The Grand Canyon.* Austin, Tex.: Raintree Steck Vaughn Publishers, 1995.

Sheridan, Thomas E. *Arizona: A History.* Tucson: University of Arizona Press, 1995.

Index

A
American Indians, 12–13, 15, 29, 36–38,
    40–45
Anglos, 12, 41, 43

B
Bright Angel Trail, 16

C
Canyon de Chelly, 13, 37, 42
Carson, Kit, 42
Central Arizona Project, 22, 25–26,
    36, 44
Chavez, Cesar, 27
Cinco de Mayo, 45
climate, 11
Coronado, Francisco Vázquez de, 39
Crook, George, 42

E
Earp, Wyatt, 43
economy, 25–30

F
Flagstaff, 14–15, 19, 28, 45

G
Gadsden Purchase, 41
Geography,
    canals, 22, 25, 36, 43–44
    canyons, 15, 19–21, 28
    dams, 19–20, 22, 44
    deserts, 11, 15, 18–19, 21–24, 25
    forests, 11, 19
    lakes, 20, 30
    mesas, 19, 28, 38
    mountains, 11, 18–19, 22–23
    plateaus, 18–19, 22–23, 37–38
    rivers, 15, 19, 22, 26, 30, 37, 43–44
Goldwater, Barry, 44
Grand Canyon, 11, 14–15, 23, 30, 39
Grey, Zane, 16
Grofe, Ferde, 16

H
Hillerman, Tony, 16
Hispanic Americans, 12, 45
history, 36–45
Holiday, Doc, 43

I
industry,
    farming, 25, 27
    high-tech companies, 12, 25, 27
    mining, 12, 25, 43

    ranching, 11
    tourism, 25, 28–30

L
Lake Havasu City, 23, 30
London Bridge, 30

M
McCain, John, 44
Meteor Crater, 15
Mexican Americans, 12, 41, 45
Mexican Independence Day, 45
Mexico, 40
Mission San Xavier del Bac, 29, 40
Mogollon Rim, 16, 19
Monument Valley, 15

N
New Spain, 40

O
Oak Creek Canyon, 15
O'Connor, Sandra Day, 35, 45
O.K. Corral, 43
Oñate, Juan de, 39

P
Painted Desert, 15
Phoenix, 12, 16, 18, 21–22, 24, 25, 27,
    29, 36, 43
population, 11, 25
Powell, John Wesley, 15

R
recreation, 11–12, 28–30, 45
Remington, Frederic, 15

S
Sedona, 15
"snowbirds," 22
state government, 31–35
Swilling, John W., 43

T
Taliesin West, 16
Treaty of Guadalupe Hidalgo, 40
Tucson, 12, 18, 22, 24, 28–29, 40

V
Valley of the Sun, 25–26

W
Wayne, John, 15
Wright, Frank Lloyd, 15–16

Y
Yuma, 24, 27